mat hekid o ju
when it rains

Volume 7

Sun Tracks

An American Indian Literary Series

mat hekid o ju
when it rains

'O'odham Ha-Cegĭtodag

Tohono O'odham and Pima Poetry

EDITED BY
OFELIA ZEPEDA

THE UNIVERSITY OF
ARIZONA PRESS
TUCSON

The University of Arizona Press
www.uapress.arizona.edu

ISBN-13: 978-0-8165-3887-4 (paper)

Cover design by Leigh McDonald
Cover photo by Kevin Dooley

Library of Congress Cataloging-in-Publication Data
Names: Zepeda, Ofelia, editor.
Title: When it rains : Tohono O'odham and Pima poetry / edited by Ofelia Zepeda.
Other titles: Sun tracks ; v. 7.
Description: Tucson : The University of Arizona Press, 2019. | Series: Sun tracks: an American Indian literary series ; volume 7
Identifiers: LCCN 2018043108 | ISBN 9780816538874 (pbk. : alk. paper)
Subjects: LCSH: Tohono O'odham poetry. | Pima poetry. | Tohono O'odham poetry—Translations into English. | Pima poetry—Translations into English.
Classification: LCC PM2174.A2 W48 2019 | DDC 897/.4552—dc23 LC record available at https://lccn.loc.gov/2018043108

Printed in the United States of America
♾ This paper meets the requirements of ANSI/NISO Z39.48-1992 (Permanence of Paper).

Contents

Foreword

Nat hab e-ju: g t-taccui?

Has our dream come true? It has been some thirty-six years since this little book, *When It Rains / Mat Hekid O Ju*, was published. Our dream at the time was to envision a flourishing contemporary written literary body for the O'odham language. At that time in history, we had speakers from all generations, and it would have been tremendous to create a contemporary literary base for those speakers. Certainly, the goal for me was to be a literate person in my first language, Tohono O'odham. One way to achieve this goal was to be part of a group that created literature for the sole purposes of sharing the aesthetic of the written word and perpetuating interest in reading and writing O'odham. This is what I was working toward at the time—practicing writing, practicing reading, and, when I could or was asked, teaching other O'odham speakers to do the same. Since that time, we've come a long way with regard to printed matter for Indigenous languages; some languages certainly have been more successful than others, though few have expanded into the realm of contemporary literature. Just as it was thirty-six years ago, most printed works in Native languages are still for teaching or other academic purposes, relegating printed Native language to these settings.

But there is something uniquely different about it now. In 1982, when this volume was originally published, the first language of the teachers whose writing appears in this collection was O'odham—and it was the same for many of their students. Though these language teachers were the bilingual in O'odham and English, most were not certified teachers but aides for their classrooms.* During

* Teresa L. McCarty and Ofelia Zepeda, "Indigenous Language Use and Change in the Americas," *International Journal of the Sociology of Language* 132 (1998).

the 1980s federal law required many reservation schools to provide funding to support students' efforts to transition from their Native languages to English. They used a bilingual approach, using both the target language (English) and the Native language to support the students' transition to English fluency.

Today the language landscape for O'odham is very different; there is no longer a need for O'odham bilingual classrooms or the bilingual method of English education. Instead, teachers move from grade to grade and room to room, bringing O'odham language and culture to the O'odham students in the schools. Some of these teachers are fluent speakers of O'odham, some are limited in their ability to speak it, and still others are second-language learners of their language. Over the last thirty-six years—the span of a generation—O'odham has suffered extreme language loss. The 1990s experienced the greatest language shift to English for many Indigenous peoples such as the O'odham.[†] This extreme shift to English and the loss of Native language has created an urgency to write the language down, to document it in all forms of media, to use it daily.

Currently, many Native American languages, like Tohono O'odham and Pima, are fading out of use. There are myriad explanations for this extreme language loss, including contact by dominant groups and other similar historical events, institutionalized religions, and educational systems generally but particularly boarding schools;[‡] the total causes are too many and complex to address here in detail. It must be noted, though, that due to both language shift and language loss, the teaching of both the oral and written forms of the O'odham language can now be found largely outside the classroom.

---

† Ofelia Zepeda and Jane H. Hill, "The Condition of Native American Languages in the United States," *Diogenes* 39, no. 153 (1991): 45–65.

‡ Michael Krauss, "The Condition of Native North American Languages: The Need for Realistic Assessment and Action," *International Journal of the Sociology of Language* 132 (1998): 9–21.

Today, many tribes must necessarily move the teaching of their languages outside the schools and into the community. These community-based teaching settings invite multiple generations to come together to learn, maintain, and revive their language. In some of these settings, the language immersion method is used; this method relies on the oral form as the primary method for language transmission, though there are a number of opportunities to create written literature in the immersion setting. But even though it is not in the school, this literature's primary purpose is to support language learning. Perhaps the best example is the case of Hawaiian language revitalization in which both oral and written language use have been promoted. Hawaiian is an exceptional case because, prior to colonization, the Hawaiian language had a rich history of writing and publication. The contemporary language revitalization movements have reached back to these early documents and have continued to add to all genres of printed literary production.[§] Aside from this unique case, other U.S. Indigenous language revitalization movements have not been as successful in actively producing much new literary material in their languages.

Despite the tremendous changes that have occurred within the O'odham languages represented in this collection, it should be noted that one thing has not changed: that is that native speakers of O'odham, those who are learning it as a second language, and all those in between are all still struck with the beauty of the language and all that it is capable of rendering. As a speaker, poet, linguist, and teacher of the Tohono O'odham language, I am still amazed by the new words and usages that I come across. The language is still so new and beautiful with each discovery we make about it, and that discovery is in how people choose to use the language as it moves and changes through time. A mere thirty-six

---

§ William H. Wilson and Kauanoe Kamanā, "Mai Loko Mai o Ka 'I'ini: Proceeding from a Dream—The 'Aha Pūnana Leo Connection in Hawaiian Language Revitalization," in *The Green Book of Language Revitalization in Practice*, ed. Leanne Hinton and Ken Hale, 147–76 (San Diego: Academic Press).

years has allowed us to witness changes in certain elements of the language—some of it good, and some not as positive. A language is allowed this flexibility to change and move according to modernity and the creativity of the people. It has always been that way.

But the changes in the language—whether good or bad—become irrelevant when O'odham gather and share the spoken words. Today, both in the Tohono O'odham Nation and in the Gila River Indian (Pima) Community, the people come together during the winter season to continue telling the story of the creation of the people and all that is around them. These gatherings are typically hosted by museums and cultural centers or other formal organizations. As always, these events are communal, and people gravitate toward them. I believe the people understand the importance of these events, even though they have changed in appearance from the events of our parents' and grandparents' times. These storytelling gatherings remind people that the real purpose of language is to perpetuate our oral history, to remind us of our origins—of who we are. Stories are capable of this. This is what I still understand to be the power of words, of language. This power that I wrote of thirty-six years ago is still there for the people, and I believe those who are now working at reclaiming spoken O'odham know this power is there in the words and that they are gaining more than just words when they learn to speak O'odham—whether it be Tohono O'odham or Pima.

Finally, I must comment on the content of the writing in this collection. The themes and experiences expressed in the writing of these people are still relevant today. While both the Tohono O'odham Nation and the Gila River Indian Community have grown and developed over time, they are still very rural communities with small villages dotting parts of the reservation; children still get bussed for miles to go to school, and their parents spend a couple of hours commuting to work each day. The rural desert environment also is still an important part of both children's and adults' lives; therefore, the themes written about thirty-six years ago are still applicable. There are words about the cycle of the seasons, about rain in the desert; there are words about the sacred mountains, and, of course, there are words of grief and loss and happiness. There are words about certain animals and about how to behave around them; many children still know of these rules. Things have changed, but many things remain the same. The pieces in this collection will be meaningful to many still.

It is important that I document here that when this collection was first released, we organized a poetry reading by the contributors of the collection. The reading was held in Sells, Arizona, the Tohono O'odham Nation's seat of government. As we made preparations for this reading, it was hard to predict what would actually happen. This was the first poetry reading ever held on the reservation. We called on many of the contributors to read their piece, and many obliged. We had an emcee for the program, and the venue was the Tohono O'odham Nation's tribal council building—the largest meeting place in Sells. It was one of the few places that had auditorium-style seating. We mailed invitations to dignitaries of the nation, school officials, and friends. We were not sure who or if anyone would come. I remember working on this with my friend and professor at the time, Larry Evers, who was then the series editor of Sun Tracks. On the day of the event, we made our way to Sells and set up for the reading. Slowly, people trickled in—adults, young people, elders, children. The auditorium was full. We shared our work, reading to a quiet and respectful audience, and afterward, as is typical with such events in the city, we served refreshments. Visiting with members from the audience and friends, I found out to my amazement that many of the tribe's businesses had closed for the afternoon so that employees could attend the event and that schools had brought busloads of students. We were overwhelmed by their support—or maybe it was their curiosity about the event. Over time, whenever I speak of this experience, I like to think of the event as one that the people knew was going to be about words, making it so important that they all should be there. Though our reading of contemporary poetry was not a telling of the origins, it was perhaps in some way just as powerful.

This collection captured the voices of a small number of language educators, representing both the Tohono O'odham Nation (at the time known as Papago) and the Pima Indians. These educators all were attending a language institute where I was their instructor. I might mention that the language institute, now known as the American Indian Language Development Institute (AILDI), is still very much active at the University of Arizona;[¶] it continues to offer courses and training to meet the needs of Native American language teachers, researchers, resource people, and activists. I have been teacher at AILDI for a long time, and the director for a number of years; during my work at AILDI, I have had the opportunity and honor to work with hundreds of language teachers from across the United States. All of them are special people—but none as special as the group whose writing is in this collection, and by my recollection, this is the first generation of literate O'odham. These educators' first language was O'odham, and they were trained to read and write in that language. They were our pioneers.

It is poignant to note that some of these educators are no longer with us. I will be saddened to know that the reissuing of this collection will bring the memory of their loved ones to their respective families. I want them to understand that I help bring the memory of their family members with respect and honor. I also want them to understand that their contribution of their *ha'icu cegitodag* to this collection was truly special. They and their words are remembered here in this work.

Ofelia Zepeda
University of Arizona
July 24, 2018

¶ Teresa L. McCarty, Lucille J. Watahomigie, Akira Y. Yamamoto, and Ofelia Zepeda, "School-Community-University Collaborations: The American Indian Language Development Institute," in *Teaching Indigenous Languages*, edited by Jon Reyhner, 85–104 (Flagstaff: Northern Arizona University, 1997).

Acknowledgments

The Native American Language Development Institute is funded by the National Endowment for the Humanities through a proposal written by Lucille Watahomigie, John Rouillard and Leanne Hinton. The purpose of the institute is to enable native speakers of native languages to get together and share their knowledge about their languages. The first institute held in 1979 consisted only of Yuman speakers. The second included Pima and Papago from the Uto-Aztecan language family. I would like to acknowledge the Native American Language Development Institute, especially directors John Rouillard and Milo Kalacteca, for enabling all of us students and teachers of the Papago and Pima language to come together to study and write. I would also like to acknowledge Coppei House Publishers and San Simon School in Sells, Arizona for allowing the use of poems which they previously printed.

Ofelia Zepeda

mat hekid o ju
when it rains

Thoughts

The power of the spoken word is great. We Papagos have always believed that, and we have always relied on powerful words in our lives. The following words are spoken as a part of a ceremony for bringing rain. This oration was spoken by "ancient ones." The words recount a journey to a place where the things of rain are stored.

Nt a hebai ep ṣoṣ
ko wa wuḍ g ñ-cewagig, am ñ-ai
am ge s-wa'usim si:bañ
T i:ya si ce:mo 'o g m-wa'aki kc am ñei
Ha'akia hewel ab ka:c, ha'akia cewagĭ ab ka:c,
    ha'akia ha'icu kaikam
ab ka:c
Pt ab da'iṣc ab dahă
T ab we:nadk ab si m-ta:t
kupt a i hoink i i:bheiwa g e-hewelig
T ab we:nadk i ha i i-juccuhimk ia dagiton ñ-jeweḍga da:m
Heg hekaj g ñ-jeweḍga am s-ke:g wa 'opagidk na:to.

The words translate something like this:

And somewhere along the way I stopped again
And it was my cloud that reached me
And it was sprinkling wetly
And here I reached your rainhouse and I looked in

There lay many winds, there lay many clouds,
    there lay many seeded things
And you set them down and sat upon them
And with them I touched you
And you moved and breathed your wind
And with it were doing things
Here you dropped it upon my land
And with that my land was sprinkled
    with water and was finished.

These spoken words are special to the rain ceremony. The people believe that in order to make the rain come they must repeat these words, these words that have been passed down from one orator to the next through many years.

I remember once listening to my mother tell of this ceremony and how it must be done in order for the rain to come. I said to her that the rain always comes at that time of year anyway. She simply replied, "that's because we always do it at that time every year." And it is true, every summer they have the ceremony and the words are repeated and one more time the rain comes. It makes me wonder what would happen if they stopped repeating the words. Some believe that when they stop reciting these words things will change. They will change and never be the same again. But the spoken words still continue now, and their power is great.

Many times the attitude that prevails among non-speakers, and even some speakers, of Indian languages is that writing down the spoken words of a language is the main means by which the language is going to be saved from extinction. I do not believe that this is true. Usually those speakers who are literate in their native languages are the very individuals who feel most secure *speaking* their language. These people look to reading and writing their language as one other means of perpetuating the use of that language, one other way that words can have power.

When the Papagos were first learning to read and write, the only printed Papago materials available were the Bible, translated by linguists and missionaries; traditional legends, transcribed by linguists; and finally, scholarly linguistics papers on Papago topics. Early language students often used the Bible as a 'text' in learning how to read Papago; many also used the legends for that same purpose. Because the linguistic papers were usually imbedded in linguistic jargon, they were difficult for native speakers to use.

Throughout the 1970s there was a movement toward self-determination in Indian communities. The move toward bilingual and bicultural education has prompted some Papagos to write and publish texts in the Papago language. These texts were usually designed for the elementary school child and therefore were very short and simple. Kept within the confines of the school these texts have had little circulation in the rest of the Papago speaking and reading community. Much the same situation exists in Pima communities.

The Papagos or Pimas who read their own language are usually employed by a school or an education program. When the move toward bilingual and bicultural education began, these were the individuals who took it upon themselves to become literate in their own language. Most are former students of a handful of Papago language experts such as: Albert Alvarez and Cipriano Manuel of the now defunct native American Language Education Project; Tony Chana of Pima Community College; Dean and Lucille Saxton; Professor Ken Hale of Massachusetts Institute of Technology; and most recently myself at the University of Arizona. Both Albert Alvarez and I have recently worked with Pima speakers. Our students are now themselves considered language teachers and linguists of the Papago language. For most, the emphasis is still on the school-age child, but it is slowly moving into the community. Some of these language teachers and linguists include: Papagos Rosilda Manuel, Helen Ramon, Daniel Lopez, and among the

Pima, Henrietta Pablo, Floretta Rhodes and Dora Miles. Under these teachers there are groups of students varying in age from five to fifty, all of them learning how to read and write their native language.

For all of us, there is still the need for more reading material. A few publications have appeared in recent years. San Simon School on the Papago Reservation has done some publications that can be used by the school-age child as well as the adult reader. Most of these consist of traditional legends or short biographical material. These materials are written in styles that are enjoyable to read, unlike some of the earlier material transcribed by non-Papago linguists. Some Papago material consisting of both songs and traditional stories as well as more contemporary writings has recently appeared in *The South Corner of Time*, volume six in *Sun Tracks*.

The poems in this collection were written during the summer of 1980 by students and teachers at the Native American Language Institute in Albuquerque, New Mexico. The institute concentrates on the language in a cultural context, as well as working with curriculum and materials development for the classroom. In this particular institute, each of the participants wrote original poetry. The initial pain of thinking of something to write was great for most of the students. Dr. Akira Yamamoto, a Yuman linguist, introduced Japanese haiku as a model. Haiku consists of very short verses, and the logic was that the students would not be intimidated by thinking that they had to write something of great length. Haiku worked with some of the students, but many were still bothered with what to write. Then one of the teachers, Helen Ramon, gave an example of a Papago poem that one of her first grade students had written. This particular poem created great enthusiasm among the students and from that time many Papago and Pima words were put down on paper. Here is a poem Elizabeth Salcido wrote as a first grader in 1974:

Mat hekid o ju:

Mat hekid o ju: t o wa'u g jeweḍ
Mat hekid o ju: t o wa'u g totoñ
Mat hekid o ju: t o ṣu:d g wo 'o
Mat hekid o ju: t o 'i: g kakawyu g ṣu:dagĭ
Mat hekid o ju: t o wuha g 'i:wagĭ
Ha 'ap at o e-ju mat hekid o ju:

When it Rains

When it rains the earth gets wet
When it rains the ants come out
When it rains the pond gets full
When it rains the horses drink water
When it rains the grass grows
That's what happens when it rains.

The words that the students put down once they got started were simple and beautiful. The words reflect emotions from one extreme to the other. They talk about life and death. They talks about happiness and sadness. There are words here about a way of life, about the times spent with grandparents and precious children. There are words here about the land that we all know so well: the desert, the saguaro cactus, the sacred mountains. There are words about the cycle of the seasons: the rain that finally falls on the desert and those clouds that finally bring the rain.

The words, as I say, are simple but beautiful. The words are also most meaningful. The meaningfulness is greatly due to the fact that the words were first thought in Papago or Pima and secondly were written in that language. Had the institute been a different one with the writing done in English, the results would, of course, have been different. I believe it would not have been as meaningful. Since we have no word for "poetry" in our language, we call poems *ha-cegĭtodag*, literally thoughts.

At the end of the institute, when the poems were shared among the participants, comments were joyful and enthusiastic. One lady remarked about Virginia Montana's words "My Brother": "It made me want to cry; I know exactly what she means." Cecelia Nuñez's poem "The Horned Toad" reminded all of the participants of when they were told to leave the horned toad alone by a grandparent.

The words and thoughts expressed in this collection of poetry do not have the same significance as the spoken words in our rain ceremony, but they do have another kind of significance. Writing thoughts in our language gives us a new choice. It gives us another way we can express ourselves. Whether the expression is in a short letter or just in writing down personal thoughts, it is thrilling to know that there is someone else out there who can read what we have put down on paper and share the experience with us. It is this new and significant and powerful experience with written words that we invite you to share here.

Papago and Pima Alphabets

PAPAGO VOWELS

a	*wako*
e	*'elidag*
i	*bit*
o	*kostal*
u	*'u:s*

In Papago all of the vowels can be pronounced long. This vowel length is marked by a colon (:).

a:	*ta:ñ*
e:	*me:*
i:	*ki:*
o:	*to:n*
u:	*hu:ñ*

Some of the vowels can be pronounced extra-short. These vowels are marked by ˘ above the vowel. These extra-short vowels usually occur only at the end of a word, as in the following examples:

bawĭ
nowĭ
hehĕ
dahă
wo:po'ŏ

PAPAGO "DIPHTHONGS"

ai	*bai*
ei	*kei*
oi	*koi*
ui	*kui*

GLOTTAL STOP

'	*'a'an, 'on*

PAPAGO CONSONANTS

b	*bo:l*
c	*ceoj*
d	*dai*
ḍ	*taḍ*
g	*ga:t*
h	*hon*
j	*je:ñ*
k	*ki:*
l	*la:mba*
m	*mu:ñ*
n	*na:k*
ñ	*ñuwĭ*
ŋ	*ca:ŋgo*
p	*pa:l*
s	*si'i*
ṣ	*ṣu:ṣk*
t	*tai*
w	*waw*
y	*ya:nda*

The Pima alphabet is the same as the Papago alphabet with the exception of a few consonants.

Where the Papago alphabet has the following:

c	*cucul*
ṣ	*ṣu:ṣk*
w	*walin*

The Pima alphabet has:

ch	*chuchul*
sh	*shu:shk*
v	*valin*

Taṣ

S-ton
    sikolk
        tonoḍ
            u:gk.

Sun

Hot
    round
        shiny
            high.

S-ke:k 'O'odham Ha-jeweḍga

Mant hekid am o ṣa 'i-oimehi am 'O'odham ha-jeweḍga ceḍ,
    an ha-ka: g 'u'uhig mo s-ke:k 'an gikuc
Mant hekid am o ṣa 'i-oimehi am 'O'odham ha-jeweḍga ceḍ,
    kg kui an gegok c an 'a'i e-wipḍut,
Mant hekid am o ṣa 'i-oimehi am 'O'odham ha-jeweḍga ceḍ,
    kg haṣañ g no:nowij 'an a hiwk wiwilin
Mant hekid am o ṣa 'i-oimehi am 'O'odham ha-jeweḍga ceḍ,
    kg ha'icu dodakam am wopo 'o kc 'am 'i-kekwup c 'i-ñ-ñeñied
Ṣag wepo mo hab cece'e, "Si att s-'ap 'i-ta:t mapt ia jiwa
    t-ki: 'am."

The Desert

When I walk in the desert
    the birds sing very beautifully
When I walk in the desert
    the trees wave their branches in the breeze
When I walk in the desert
    the tall saguaro wave their arms way up high
When I walk in the desert
    the animals stop and look at me as if they were saying
"Welcome to our home."

'O'odham Mu:sigo

M'añ ñeidc ka: g 'O'odham Mu:sigo,
    k a'm s-hemajim gew g wioli:ñ,
Kc 'an s-ba:bgim wañ'on g 'a:lgo,
    kc hab wua mo s-'i 'owim ñe'e g wawñim wainom,
Kc 'an s-haukam himcud g 'e-nowĭ,
    kc hab wua mo g ñ-wui ñeok g ñe'edam 'u:s,
Kc heg hab wua mo g ñ-'i:bdag s-he:kigam kowoḍ,
    hab masma mo g ju:kĭ hab wua g ha:ṣañ 'i:bdag,
T hebai o ṣa hi: g 'O'odham Mu:sigo,
    nt 'am o a 'i 'oidc o ka:kc cem hekid o s-hemajmakad.

Papago Music

Whenever I see and hear the Papago Music
    and the violin is played so nicely
And the bow goes back and forth so slowly,
    and it seems that the strings are singing to me so sweetly,
And the hand moves back and forth so lightly,
    and it seems as if the singing bow is speaking to me,
And it seems to cause my heart to beat with joy,
    just like the saguaro's heart when the rain finally comes,
Where ever the Papago Music goes,
    I will follow it and listen to it and I will always be a happy person.

—

Mant hekid am o ha shulik hi:
g ñ-ve:m ki:kam
k hab ta:hadag mant ha'ichu si hephu wa:
Nt eḍa am va o u:pam o hi:

When I leave my family
I feel like I've really lost a special
Part of me
But I know I will always return.

Ñ-lu'u

Ñ-lu'u 'o wuḍ oks
haṣ ba s-ma:c g huata
we:s taṣkaj at o huat
am 'o mu'i ha-na:to c 'o ha gagda
hagac o ui g lo:nji
hab masma 'o s-kowok g ñ-lu'u

My Grandmother

My grandmother is old
But she knows how to make baskets
She makes baskets all day,
When she finishes a lot, she sells them
With the money she buys groceries
In this way my grandmother never goes hungry.

Haṣañ

Ṣa:cu ap ñeid ab hasañ ab?
ñeid ap g bahidaj
ñeid ap g sitol
ñeid ap g lu:lsi
ñeid ap g nawait
Hab a hegai am si taṣo mo ḍ 'O'odham himdag.

Saguaro

What do you see in a saguaro cactus?
you see its fruits
you see its syrup
you see its candy
you see its wine
but most of all you see Papago tradition.

Wi'ikam Do'ag

Wi'ikam Do'ag
Wi'ikam Do'ag
gan hu si s-ap masma an ke:k
heg da:m g huhugam 'o 'odham an ki:kahim

Lonely Mountain

Lonely Mountain
Lonely Mountain
Over there it stands so finely
On top of this lonely mountain
    "the disappeared people" once lived.

'Oks Dahă

'Oks Da:kam Du'ag
'Oks Da:kam Du'ag
Gam hu huḍnig ta:gio si s-ap 'am ku:gam dahă
Ṣa:cu 'ap has wua kc 'am ku:gam dahă?

Lady Sitting Mountain

Lady Sitting Mountain,
Lady Sitting Mountain,
Over there towards the west you sit so finely with your back to us.
What are you doing sitting there with your back towards us?

—

ʼA:ñi ʼañ s-hohoid mant o cipkan
ʼA:ñi ʼañ s-hohoid mant o ñeʼed
ʼA:ñi ʼañ s-hohoid mant o wapkon g ñ-eʼeñga
ʼA:ñi ʼañ s-hohoid mant o kekc g ñ-ki:
ʼA:ñi ʼañ s-hohoid mant o hihidod
ʼA:ñi ʼañ s-hohoid g ñ-keliga.

I like to work.
I like to sing.
I like to wash my clothes.
I like to clean my house.
I like to cook.
I like my old man.

Mañ eḍa al cemaj

Mañ eḍa al cemaj añ am ki: Ce:co tam
Mañ eḍa al camaj añ ñ-maṣcam
Mañ eḍa al cemaj añ wi:p g wihog
Mañ eḍa al cemaj añ 'u'u g uṣap
Mañ eḍa al cemaj añ 'u'u g ṣegai
Kc Hemu g 'a'al pi b ṣa'i e-wua

When I Was Small

When I was small I lived in Chui-Chui.
When I was small I went to school.
When I was small I chewed on mesquite beans.
When I was small I picked dry sap.
When I was small I picked greasewood.
And now children don't do this any more.

’O’odham Ñe’i A:ga

’O ’odham ñeñe’i ’o amjeḍ ñe’e
    heg jeveḍ
    heg mu:kik
    heg pig elidag
    heg himdag
’o ve:s ’e-ve:m hihim ’id jeveḍ ka:chim.

Pima Song

Pima song tells of long ago
    it tells about land
    it tells about death
    it tells about love
    it tells about living
All in harmony with nature.

'Ali

'Ali 'o s-ke:g e-ñeid
mat hegid 'o s-he:kik
masma mat g baihidaj
si s-ke:g o bai k si
s-'iowim 'o ma:sk.

A Baby

A baby is beautiful
When he is happy
Just like a saguaro fruit,
When it is ripe
And looks good.

Ceoj Ñ-we:nag

'O 'ohana 'at am gei
ñ-o:g 'o ṣuak
ñ-je'e 'o ṣuak
ñ-wepnag 'o ṣuak
a:ñi 'añ ṣuak
'o 'ohana 'at b t-ju:,
We:s g t-o: 'ogĭ 'o e-iawad
'ali ñ-we:nag 'o pi amicud
        "Ṣa: t e-ju:?"
        "Ṣa: t e-ju:?"
'o 'ohana at am gei,
ceoj ñ-we:nag atṣ nhu b 'i-e-ju:
pi att hegid o ṣa'i pi m-cekto
s-'ap e-ta:tkad 'an t-da:m ka:cim 'ab
heg hegaj matt hema taṣgaj o m-ñei
pi att hegid o ṣa'i pi m-cekto.

My Brother

A letter came.
My father is crying,
My mother is crying,
My brothers and sisters are crying,
I am crying.
A letter caused this.
Our tears are pouring.
My baby brother doesn't understand it:
    "What happened?"
    "What happened?"
A letter did this to us.
My brother has passed away.
We will never forget you.
Be happy in heaven.
Someday we will see you.
We will never forget you.

Ṣopol Eṣabig Maṣad

Ju:kĭ,
hewel,
si s-'ap hab 'u:wĭ
'ep ṣa s-hewog
nt 'am 'eḍa o me:
k 'ep 'am 'eḍa o hi:
t 'im huh ab o e-ju: g pi 'ap tahadkam.

August

Rain,
Wind,
Smells so good,
It makes me sort of cold.
I run outside,
To walk in it
And all my troubles go away.

Pi g 'an hu ta:tam

"Dakton g cemamagĭ!"
ñ-hu'ul 'o hab kaij.
Kupt hab e-elid mant 'an o ta:t?
        S-wepegĭ wu:pui
cew ñe:ñ,
        s-hiwk
Cemamagĭ, pi g an hu ñ-miabidad.

Don't Touch

"Leave the horned toad alone!"
My grandmother said.
Does she think I want to touch him?
    Red eyes,
long tongue,
    rough skin,
Horned toad, leave me alone.

Da:m Ka:cim

S-cuhugam

'Ab 'o him,

S-ba:bagĭ 'o 'ab him.

Huhu'u

'An dadhă,

Kc ñ-ñu:kut,

C ñ-ta:gio 'am tonolid.

Maṣad

'Ab ceṣajim,

mat 'am 'o 'i ñ-tonol.

Ko:ṣ

Ko:sig 'añ ta:tk

S-'ap hab ta:tadag.

Taṣ

Kia'a koi'o

Pi g ab hu kia 'i be: g taṣ.

Sky

Night

here it comes,
it comes gradually.

Stars

there they are,
they watch over me.

Moon

she's coming up,
coming to light my way.

Sleep

I feel it,
it feels so good,

Sun

wait sun,
hold back the day.

Hevel

Hevel 'o ab meḍ,
kus hebai o me:
kus habai amjeḍ meḍ
pi hedai sha'i ma:ch.

Wind

The wind is coming,
Wonder where it is going
And where is it coming from?
Nobody knows.

Mañ ap meḍ Albuquerque wui
añ am ñeid si mu'i s-ke:g
ha'icu mo g jeveḍ ka:chim b ma:s
'id amjeḍ si ge'e has elda hab e-ju:.

On my way to Albuquerque
I see many beautiful desert scenes,
Mountains, rivers, cliffs and trees.
All were gleaming in their unique ways.
How grateful I felt to Mother Earth.

Ha'a

bid

o 'od

ṣu:dagĭ

s-ke:gaj.

Olla

earth
    pebbles
        water
            pretty.

Ñ-hu'ul

Ñ-hu'ul 'o hab masma mo g ñ-je'e
ñ-hu'ul 'o wuḍ we:s he'icu mañ eḍegid
ha'icu 'apedag 'a:ga 'o wuḍ ñ-hu'ul
ñ-maṣcamdag 'o wuḍ ñ-hu'ul
ñ-a'alga ha-wi:kol 'o wuḍ ñ-hu'ul
hemuc 'añ cem hekid cekto g ñ-hu'ul
hemuc 'o pi ha'icuk g ñ-hu'ul
pi 'ap
tahadkam.

My Grandmother

My grandmother is like my mother.
My grandmother is everything that I own.
Everything that is good is my grandmother.
My education is my grandmother.
My children's greatgrandmother is my grandmother.
Now I am longing for my grandmother.
sorrow.

Tohono

Tohono 'o wuḍ t-ki:
amai mo g haṣañ mu'ic
c g ṣeṣgai s-ce:dagĭ
c s-ap hab u:w
Tohono 'o wuḍ bahidaj,
i:bhai, ciolim, wihog
Tohono 'o wuḍ mu'i t-wahudag
c t-apedag
Tohono 'o wuḍ t-duagak.

Desert

The desert is our home.
There where saguaro are many,
Where greasewood is green,
Smelling nice.
The desert is cactus fruit,
Prickly pear, cholla, mesquite beans.
The desert is work, but for our good
The desert is for our good.

Toniab

Mat g toniabkam 'o e-a'ahe,
t g ju:kĭ o jiwia
t g ṣa'i kc kui o s-ce:dagi
t we:s g jewed (t-je'e) 'o s-ce:dagi k.

S-he:bijedkam

Mat g s-he:bĭ o jiwia,
t g gew o gei,
t o gewai g jeweḍ
k g ṣa'i o gagṣ
t g kui ha:hag o ko 'o.

Summer

When summer is here,
the rain is here,
the grass and the trees become green,
and the whole mother earth is green.

Winter

When the winter is here,
the snow is here
the ground turns dry,
and the leaves from the trees die.

’Eḍa Hukkam Maṣad

Mat ’eḍa hukkam ’o ṣu:d g maṣad
kut gahu ’u:gk o dakad c hab
’o ñ-ñeidad
k hab wuḍ ’a:ga mat o ju:kad si’alim

Mat o ṣu:d g maṣad

Mat hekid o ṣu:d g maṣad
’at o ge kawoḍka g maṣad
k hab wuḍ ’a:ga
mat o heweḍad si’alim.

Quarter Moon

A quarter moon standing tall,
looking down at me,
a rainy tomorrow

Full Moon

When there is a full moon
a circle surrounds it,
the meaning of it is
a windy tomorrow.

Hemho Añ Am Him

Hemho ant am ve:m hi: g ñ-sho'igdag
Nt am bek g ñ-sho'igdag
Am akimel wui k am hava hephu wa:.

Once I Walked

Once I walked with sadness,
I walked to the river.
My sadness was lost.

Ira

Hegam Pi:ma
at si has el g Ira
mat am 'i-cheshaj
g vanjel am da:m g Iwo Jima.

Ira

How proud the Pimas
when Ira raised the flag
at Iwo Jima.

Taḍai

Taḍai, taḍai
bapt o me:?
s-meldag ʼa:pi ba añ ma m-ñeid
ṣapt e-ju: k hab ʼan si has ñenhog?
nap a:ñi an ñ-ga:k?
. . . . . . ʼi añ hu ke:k.

Roadrunner

Roadrunner, roadrunner,
Where are you running to?
Fast you are, but I've seen you.
What did you do? That's why you're looking around.
Are you looking for me?
. . . . . . I'm standing over here.

Ha:ṣañ

Ha:ṣañ 'o 'in hab ke:k ñ-ki: hugid an.
Cewaj 'o i:da kc 'ep s-ho'idag.
Ḍ 'o t-eṣ c wuḍ ep t-nawaj.
Nam ka: maṣ g ha:ṣañ hab ba ep
    wuḍ 'o'odham?
A:ñi 'añ hi ka: kc hab si has e:lid.

Saguaro Cactus

A saguaro cactus stands by my house
It is long and has thorns.
It is our plant and also our friend.
Did you hear that the saguaro cactus is also 'O'odham?
I heard, and I truly respect it.

Ñeñe'i

Ñeñe'i, ñeñe'i,
Idam 'o s-ke:g wuḍ ha'icu.
Mapt hekid pi ap o e-ta:tkad
    t u:gk o 'i bei g m-i:bdag
Mapt hekid o s-he:kig
    t am ba'ic o 'i si u:gk 'i m-beic.
Mapt has o 'i e-ta:tkad,
    k g ñe'i hab 'o ṣa we:nad
    t s-ke:g wuḍ 'o ha'icuk.

Songs

Songs, songs,
They are something special.
When you're feeling low,
They will lift your spirits.
When you're happy,
They will lift your spirits even more.
However you feel,
Whenever you put a song with it,
You'll find they are something special.

Do:da'ag

Do:da'ag 'o 'an t-bi:ṣc
na:nko 'o mams 'idam.
Ha'i 'o wuḍ i'akcul do:da'ag
milga:n 'o ia daiwup c ha-paḍjud 'idam
K hascu a:g hab e-wua
k eḍa wuḍ si ha'icu idam?

Giho Du'ag 'o an ke:k,
Waw Giwulk 'o an ke:k,
Winta:na 'o an ke:k,
Mu'ic 'o idam
t hu'i an habṣ 'o gegokad.

Mountains

Mountains surround us.
Various shapes and colors, they are.
Some of them are sacred mountains.
Whitemen come and they destroy them.
Why do they do this?
Yet they are very dear to us.

Giho Du'ag stands there,
Waw Giwulk stands there,
Winta:na stands there.
There are many of these.
I wish they would just stand there, untouched.

Piast

Mat g wainom kuikud am o ku
t si'iskol o e-waila g e-wailadam
t g ku:ps o 'i-wu:ṣ
t g kuidas o kokp
k 'id wuḍ piast

Mat g e-wañohondam am o e-ge:g
t g hemajkam o e-co:di
t g 'a'al ab o ñenad
ko 'okol am e-hihidod
k 'id wuḍ piast

Mat g gidal am o e-ge:g
t g hemajkam o e-kuali:ya
t g kakanjul o me:mhet
t ia o e-nam g e-nanwoj
k 'id wuḍ piast

Mat g tatamblo o kaida
t o e-waila g e-wailadam
k g so:la o e-i:
t g na:da o ku:phoñid
k 'id wuḍ piast

Mat g ge 'e gidal am o e-ge:g
t g hemajkam o e-masu:laga
t g taṣ ab o 'i-ceṣ
t am aṣ o kia e-piastad
k 'id wuḍ piast.

Chicken Scratch

When the saxophone plays
And the dancers whirl
the dust flies
And the firecrackers burst
It's a chicken scratch dance!

When the accordion plays
And the dancers glide
the children stare
And the red chili cooks
It's a chicken scratch dance!

When the guitar plays
And the dancers two-step
and the lights flicker
And friends meet
It's a chicken scratch dance!

When the drums play
And the dancers polka
the drinks flow
And the fires smoke
It's a chicken scratch dance!

When the bass guitar plays
And the dancers cumbia
the sun comes up
And the dancing goes on
It's a chicken scratch dance!

Ju:kĭ

ʼIm ʼat hu ʼi-e-ju: g taṣ
kia, ṣaʼi si s-tonĭ
we:s haʼicu ʼan ʼaṣ ʼi pi hoiñag
mumuwal s-ba:big ʼan daʼa
we:s haʼicu ʼat ʼi-e-ba:bigi.

Ñ-o:g ʼo ʼab dahă
si taʼi mo ʼok c ko:ṣ
ñ-we:nag ʼo gnhu wo ʼo kc ko:ṣ
gogs ʼat ʼam bij ki: we:big
ʼe:heg ʼo an ga:k
we:s haʼicu ʼat ʼi-ba:bigi

Tk ʼeḍa pi ṣa:muñhim an
ʼi-daḍhiwa
g cewagĭ
ju: ʼat! ju: ʼat!
daʼiwuṣ ʼat g ñ-o:g
"meḍ k am maʼiṣp g ñ-pilkan"
"meḍ k ʼu:ʼi g ʼe-hehl̵iga"
We:s haʼicu ʼat hahawa ʼi-hoi
ju: ʼat, ju: ʼat!
daʼiwuṣ ʼat g ñ-we:nag
daʼiwuṣ ʼat g gogs
we:s haʼicu ʼat hahawa ʼi-hoi.

Rain

The sun has moved down that way a bit,
And yet it is so hot.
All movement has almost stopped.
A fly goes by so slowly,
everything has slowed down.
My father is sitting there,
His head is tilted back and he's asleep.
My sister is laying over there, asleep.
The dog passed by, he is looking
for shade,
everything has slowed down.
And yet the clouds have slowly settled in.
It's raining, it's raining!
My father jumps up
"Run and cover my grain!"
"Run and get the clothes on the line!"
Everything is now moving and alive.
My sister is up,
The dog is up,
everything is now moving and alive.

Ḍ'ac 'O'odham

Gan 'at hu 'i 'e-ju: g taṣ
ga 'at hu 'i hihi g cewagĭ'
ṣa'i si s-to:ta
ṣa'i si ge'egḍaj
'ac 'ia daḍhă c ñenda g ju:kĭ

'Ab 'o hihim g cewagĭ
'u'ua 'o g ju:kĭ
ḍ 'o 'Kaij Cukalig Maṣad'
An 'ac u:gk ha'icu ñeid c ñenda g ju:kĭ

'Ab 'o hihim g cewagĭ
s-ap 'o u:wĭ g ju:kĭ
s-hewog 'o g hewel
s-ap 'ac tahadag c 'ia ñenda g ju:kĭ

'Ab 'o hihim g cewagĭ
'an 'at 'aṣ bi:bij g cewagĭ
pi 'atkĭ o ṣa'i ju:
t 'iatokĭ 'at g cewagĭ
ḍ 'ac 'O'odham c 'ia daḍhă c ñenda g ju:kĭ

We Are Papago

The sun has moved over a bit that way.
Here come the clouds.
They are so very white,
They are so very big,
As we sit here and wait for the rain.

Here come the clouds.
They are carrying the rain.
It is the Seed Blackening Month,
As we look up in the skies and wait for the rain.

Here come the clouds.
The rain smells good.
The breeze is refreshingly cool.
We feel happy as we wait for the rain.

Here come the clouds.
But the clouds have just gone by.
It is not going to rain.
The clouds have lied to us.
We are the Papago and se sit here and wait for the rain.

Afterword

This volume of Pima and Papago poetry represents one of the most important recent developments in the arts and humanities in this country—namely, the growth of new traditions of creating writing in Native American languages. The expressive power and beauty of these languages has been recognized for centuries, both by native speakers of the languages and by outsiders who have had the good fortune to learn something of them. For various reasons, however, this extraordinarily rich intellectual resource has not been permitted to assume its rightful place in the intellectual lives of the people who speak them or the country's population at large. That role is central in the education and general intellectual activities of the people who speak them natively. If their rightful role were permitted to Native American languages, the country as a whole would be enriched.

Unhappily for this country, though we are by no means alone, severe and relatively constant linguistic oppression has been directed against indigenous peoples. Only by virtue of great courage and steadfastness of enduring Native American communities is there, in many parts of the country, still an opportunity to reverse the situation that has prevailed so long. This reversal, if it takes place, will not be won without a struggle. It is thus of great importance that the support for Native American linguistic rights be marshalled in all quarters where people accept the premise that linguistic and cultural pluralism is essential to ensuring the fullest possible expression of the human intellectual capacity.

For this reason, as much as for their intrinsic beauty and gemlike quality, are poems written by native speakers of Papago and Pima so precious and important. The poems in this volume are not only an invitations to fellow Piman speakers and to the world to appreciate the expressive force of the language. They are also a small but concrete demonstration of the promise which lies within the language and which could be realized if the language were allowed to assume its role in the intellectual life of the Piman people.

Although the genre represented in these poems is new, the writing of Pima and Papago by native speakers is of some historical depth. This poetry, therefore, continues an honorable tradition. Perhaps the earliest Piman person to write extensively in his native language was the Papago, Jose Lewis (also known as Jose Lewis Brennan), who, among a variety of noteworthy accomplishments, set down in writing the bulk of the Pima textual material in Frank Russell's *The Pima Indians*, appearing originally in the *Twenty-sixth Annual Report of the Bureau of Ethnology, 1904-1905* and republished in 1975 by the University of Arizona Press. This impressive work remains an extremely important source of linguistic and ethnographic data. Another writer to whom we owe an enormous intellectual debt is the late Juan Dolores, who began in 1911 to write down Papago legends, with a view to eventually publishing them and making them available to other speakers of Papago. Many of his writings were eventually published in the excellent volume *Legends and Lore of the Papago and Pima Indians*, compiled by Dean and Lucille Saxton and published in 1973 by the University of Arizona Press. In addition to these traditional texts, Dolores also produced two valuable grammatical studies and an essay on Papago nicknames. The linguistic sensitivity which Dolores displayed has contributed much to the understanding we now have of Papago grammar.

In the present period, the work and writings of Albert Alvarez are particularly worthy of note. His two essays *'O'odham Ñe'okĭ ha-Kaidag* (The Sounds of Papago) and *'O'odham Ñe'okĭ he-Ce'idag* (The Expression of Papago), to my knowledge at least, comprise the first linguistic treatises *in* an indigenous language of North America. These have not been published in full, but parts of them appear as an appendix to my essay "A new perspective no American Indian linguistics," in Alfonso Ortiz, *New Perspectives on the Pueblos*, published in 1972 by the University of Arizona Press. Alvarez is also responsible for the transcriptions appearing in Bahr, et al., *Piman Shamanism and Staying Sickness (Ka:cim Mumkidag)*, University of Arizona Press, 1973, and for the transcription of the long Papago creation story, part of which appeared in the *Sun Tracks* volume entitled *The South Corner of Time*. Alvarez has also written numerous other works in connection with his work in Papago language literacy. Due in large measure to his efforts, a significant number of Papago speakers have become literate in Papago and have contributed to the foundations of a written literature in the language. It is in the orthography used by Alvarez in his teaching and writing that the poems of this volume are written.

An especially important event in the recent history of Papago language scholarship has been the advent of Ofelia Zepeda, editor of this volume. In addition to her impressive linguistic and literary talents, she has brought with her an extraordinarily clear vision of the educational potential which her native language possesses, together with a firm commitment to seeing that the Papago language occupies its proper place in the education of Papago children and young adults. Her resolve can be appreciated from the fact that she has assumed responsibility for Papago language and literacy courses while, at the same time, working toward her degree in one of the best and most demanding graduate linguistics programs in the country. From the very beginning she recognized the importance of creative writing to the goals toward which she and other Native American linguists are striving. If literacy is essential in the effort to define a central and persisting educational role for a language, then creative writing is also an essential ingredient, because literacy depends, at least party, upon literature. This is the perspective which Zepeda brought to the summer workshops in which she taught, and it is due in no small measure to her vision that the poems included in this volume are here to enjoy.

In short, this books fits into a much larger scheme, part dream and part reality. It is a part of a real tradition involving the writing of Piman, albeit a tradition of as yet relatively few practitioners. But it promises much more—the flowering of a written literature fully portraying the Piman experience, the hardship and sorrow, as well as the grace and beauty. That is the dream.

Ken Hale

M.I.T.

Cambridge, Mass.

About the Editor

OFELIA ZEPEDA is a Tohono O'odham poet, a regents' professor of linguistics at the University of Arizona, and the recipient of a MacArthur Fellowship for her work in American Indian language education. She is the author of a grammar of the Tohono O'odham language, *A Tohono O'odham Grammar* (University of Arizona Press, 1983), and her poetry collections include Ocean Power: Poems from the Desert (University of Arizona Press, 1995), *Jewed'l-hoi/Earth Movements, O'Odham Poems* (Kore, 2005), and *Where Clouds Are Formed* (University of Arizona Press, 2008).